NFL TODAY

THE STORY OF THE CLEVELAND BROWNS

THE STORY OF THE CLEVELAND BROWNS

SARA GILBERT

CREATIVE EDUCATION

Cover: Running back Jim Brown (top), tight ends
Kellen Winslow Jr. and Steve Heiden (bottom)
Page 2: Quarterback Otto Graham
Pages 4–5: Coach Blanton Collier
Pages 6–7: Quarterback Brady Quinn

....

Published by Creative Education
P.O. Box 227, Mankato, Minnesota 56002
Creative Education is an imprint of
The Creative Company
www.thecreativecompany.us

Design and production by Blue Design
Design Associate: Sarah Yakawonis
Printed in the United States of America

Photographs by Getty Images (Kimberly Barth/
AFP, J. Baylor Robers/National Geographic, Al Bello/
Allsport, Scott Boehm, Diamond Images, Stephen
Dunn, Focus On Sport, George Gojkovich, Bob
Gomel/Time & Life Pictures, Henry Barr Collection/
Diamond Images, Ross Lewis/NFL, Ronald C. Modra/
Sports Imagery, NFL, Hy Peskin/Sports Illustrated,
Pro Football Hall Of Fame/NFL, Art Rickerby/
Diamond Images, George Rose, Gregory Shamus,
Paul Spinelli, Matt Sullivan, Tony Tomsic, Tony
Tomsic/NFL, Jim Turner/NFL, Ron Vesely)

Library of Congress Cataloging-in-Publication Data

Gilbert, Sara.
The story of the Cleveland Browns / by Sara Gilbert.
p. cm. — (NFL today)
Includes index.
ISBN 978-1-58341-752-2
1. Cleveland Browns (Football team: 1946–1995)
—History—Juvenile literature. I. Title. II. Series.

GV956.C6G56 20085082
796.332'640977132—dc22   2008022683

First Edition
9 8 7 6 5 4 3 2 1

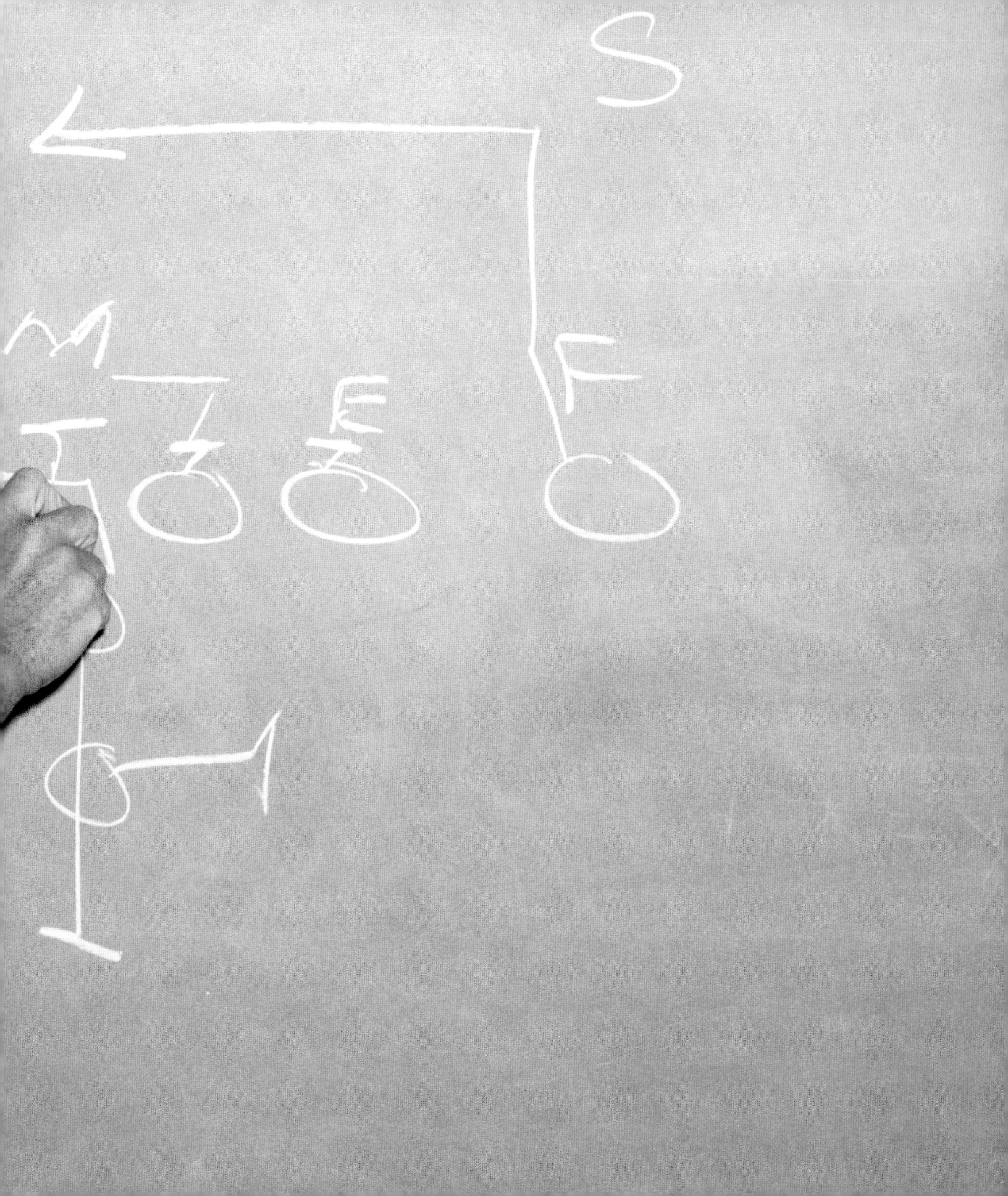
S
M
E
F

CONTENTS

ON THE SIDELINES

MEET THE BROWNS

BROWN LEADS THE BROWNS

Cleveland, Ohio, was founded on the southern shore of Lake

Erie in 1796. Because of its easy access to waterways and

railroad lines, the bustling port city soon became a major

manufacturing hub. As steel was shipped out of its foundries

to points around the globe, Cleveland earned a reputation

as a hard-working, industrial city. Although that description

still applies, Cleveland is now a modern metropolis also known

as the home of the Rock and Roll Hall of Fame and the Great

Lakes Science Center.

X Famous for
its heavy industry,
Cleveland has been
known as one of the
United States' most
important steel and
iron processing centers
since the days of the
American Civil War.

The city is also known for the Cleveland Browns, the

National Football League (NFL) franchise that was first

founded as a member of the All-America Football Conference

(AAFC) in 1946. The people of the city selected the team's

name in honor of one of their own: Paul Brown, a beloved

college coach who was picked to serve as the team's first

leader. Since then, the Browns have built a reputation for

being as tireless and loyal as the fans who support them.

When he built the first Browns team, coach Paul Brown

allowed the lessons he'd learned from his days at the college

level to guide him. He recruited several of his former players,

including kicker Lou "The Toe" Groza, and went after others

whom he had admired as opponents, including lanky receiver

Mac Speedie and fullback Marion Motley. But his greatest

achievement was in signing quarterback Otto Graham from Chicago's Northwestern University.

With Brown's handpicked roster, Cleveland emerged as the AAFC's most fearsome team. The Browns compiled an incredible 52–4–3 record in the league's four-year history, going undefeated in 1948 and winning all four championships. Still, few people believed that the team could continue that success when the Browns became part of the NFL in 1950.

Coach Brown believed in his team. But to convince everyone else of their capabilities, the Browns had to defeat the defending NFL champion Philadelphia Eagles in the first game of the 1950 season. The underdog Browns scored a touchdown on their first offensive possession—a 59-yard touchdown pass from Graham to speedy receiver Dub Jones—and never looked back. Graham threw for 346 yards and launched 2 more touchdown passes as the Browns embarrassed the Eagles 35–10. "We were so fired up," Graham remembered. "We would have played them for a keg of beer or a chocolate milk shake."

With the help of powerful defensive end Len Ford and center Frank Gatski, the Browns put together a 10–2 season that culminated in a 30–28 victory over the Los Angeles Rams in the NFL Championship Game. Cleveland went on to win the

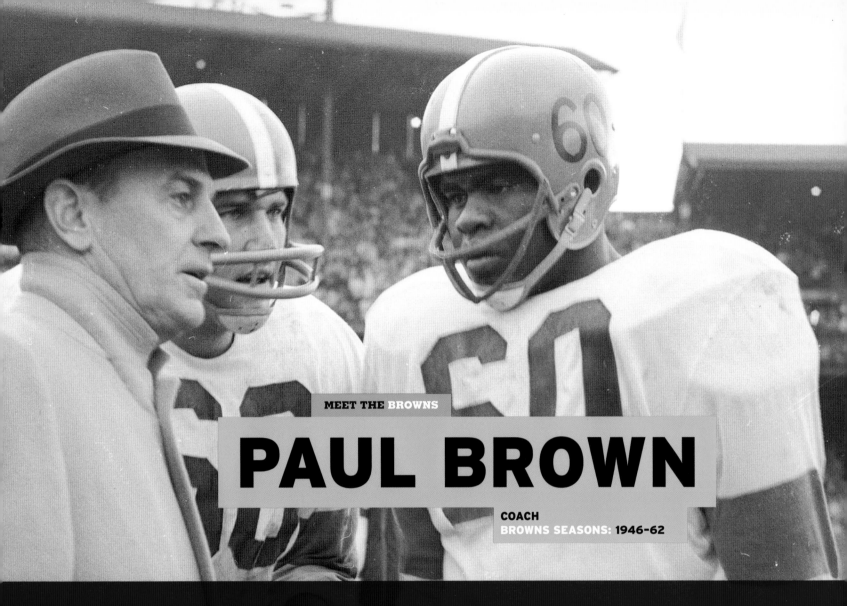

PAUL BROWN

COACH
BROWNS SEASONS: 1946-62

Paul Brown could have become a lawyer. Instead, he became a football coach—one of the greatest of all time. His first coaching job was at a naval academy prep school in Maryland, where he compiled a record of 16–1–1 in two years. That success was enough to make Brown scrap his plans for law school and put his energies into coaching instead. Before long, the Ohio native had moved up to the college ranks and, in 1945, was asked to lead the brand-new Cleveland Browns team. But Brown was hardly a traditional coach. In addition to using intelligence tests to screen potential players, he also built a library of game film and studied it regularly. A former teacher, he herded his players into classrooms for instruction and used a radio transmitter to communicate with players on the field. Brown's tactics broke new ground at the time and helped him assemble a 167–53–8 record during his 17 seasons with the Browns. "He's certainly one of the key figures in professional sports," said Cincinnati Bengals quarterback Ken Anderson. "Football would not be what it is without him."

NAMING THE BROWNS

The first order of business after Arthur "Mickey" McBride purchased a professional football franchise for Cleveland was to find it a coach—and McBride quickly fixed on local hero Paul Brown, who had led Ohio State University to a national college championship in 1942. The next item on the agenda was to select a name for the team—but as it turned out, that went right along with finding its coach. McBride offered a $1,000 war bond to the person who could select the best name for the team. Many of the entries suggested that the team be called the Browns, in honor of its beloved coach. But that made Paul Brown uncomfortable, and McBride instead paid the $1,000 to a fan who had recommended "Cleveland Panthers." Unfortunately, that didn't work either; an NFL team had used that name in 1926 and still owned the rights. McBride went back to the fans' first choice: the Cleveland Browns. Although Paul Brown maintained that the name was in honor of boxer Joe "The Brown Bomber" Louis, he later acknowledged that it was for him instead.

NFL Eastern Conference title for five more years, capturing two more league championships in 1954 and 1955. The NFL Championship Game against the Rams in 1955 was Graham's last; after throwing two touchdowns and running for two more, he left the game to a standing ovation from the fans at Los Angeles Memorial Coliseum.

Graham's departure left a gaping hole at quarterback and ushered in the Browns' first losing season, a 5–7 campaign in 1956. But it also opened the door for a new superstar to emerge in Cleveland: running back Jim Brown, a 6-foot-2 and 232-pound powerhouse drafted by the Browns in 1957. With a frightening combination of speed and strength, he ran for 942 yards and scored 9 touchdowns as a rookie. The following

X Marion Motley (number 76), who became one of the first African American stars in pro football in the 1940s, led the Browns as both a steamrolling fullback and a punishing linebacker.

X Although running back Ernie Green (right) was an NFL star in his own right, playing in two Pro Bowls, he spent most of his Browns career in the shadow of the great Jim Brown.

year, he nearly doubled those numbers. Before the end of his NFL career, Brown would gain 12,312 total yards, score 106 touchdowns, and win an incredible 8 league rushing titles.

Brown's running heroics took some of the pressure off the string of quarterbacks, including Milt Plum, who tried to replace Graham. The team rode atop Brown's shoulders to win the division in 1957 and, with the help of receiver Ray Renfro, made it to the playoffs again in 1958. In 1959, Brown led the NFL with 1,329 rushing yards, and in 1960, Plum threw 21 touchdowns, but the team missed the playoffs both times.

Although the Browns compiled winning records each of the next two seasons, they failed to bring another title home to Cleveland. For a team accustomed to championships, the late 1950s and early '60s were disappointing, and owner David Jones sold the Browns to former television producer Art Modell in 1961. Almost immediately, Modell clashed with

OTTO GRAHAM

QUARTERBACK
BROWNS SEASONS: 1946-55
HEIGHT: 6-FOOT-1
WEIGHT: 196 POUNDS

Illinois native Otto Graham went to Chicago's Northwestern University on a basketball scholarship. One day, the football coach saw him throwing a football for fun and talked him into joining the team. That decision launched a Hall of Fame career that would span 10 years and include 3 NFL and 4 AAFC championships. Graham was one of the premier quarterbacks of his era, throwing 174 career touchdowns and being elected to the Pro Bowl 5 times. Graham's dominance on the gridiron was so complete that when he announced his retirement after the 1954 season, coach Paul Brown begged him to return. In Graham's encore season, he led the Browns to a 9–2–1 record and a 38–14 victory over the Los Angeles Rams in the NFL Championship Game on December 26, 1955. Upon his death in 2003, Graham was described as "an absolute model of character and integrity" by Hall of Fame president John Bankert. He is widely considered one of the greatest football players of all time, and his number 14 jersey is one of only 5 that have been retired by the Browns.

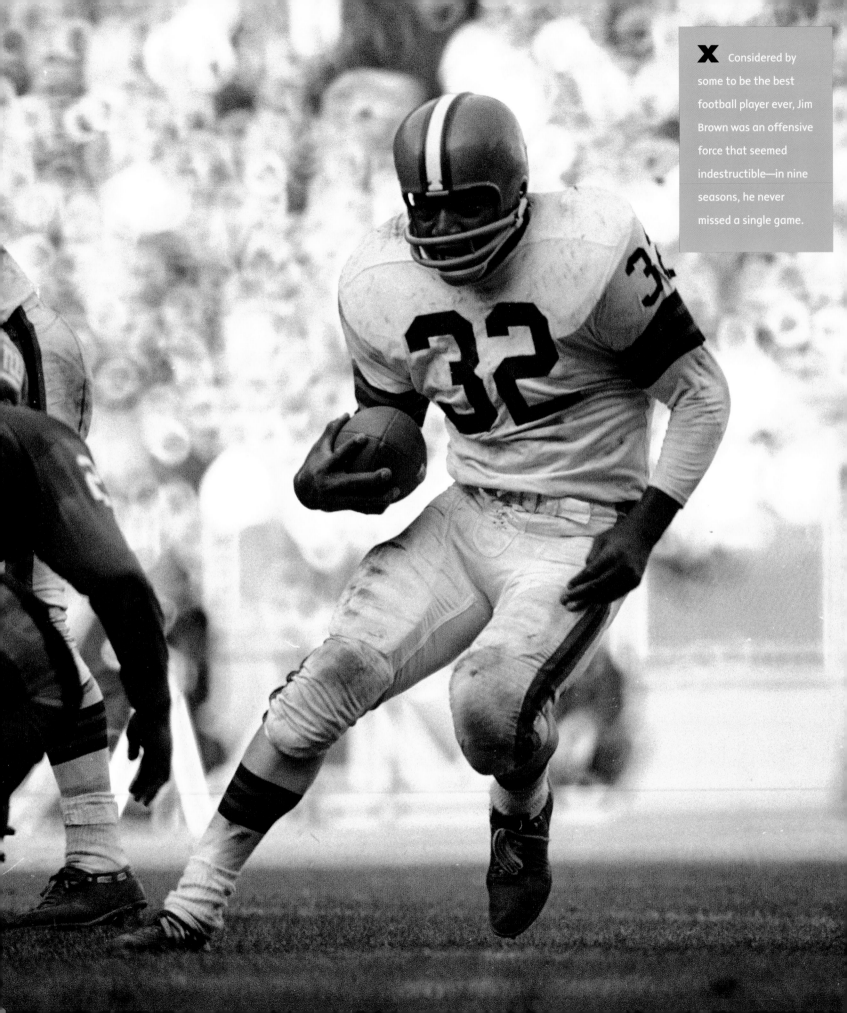

Coach Brown, whose no-nonsense style had also rubbed some younger players, including Jim Brown, the wrong way.

When the 1962 season ended with a disappointing 7–6–1 record, Modell fired the popular coach. Although Brown was asked to stay on as an adviser, he soon quietly disappeared and later started another professional football team in Ohio, the Cincinnati Bengals. Brown, who had been known as one of the best coaches in the game, bitterly referred to his tenure under Modell as "the darkest period in my life."

X Guard Gene Hickerson spent his entire 15-year NFL career in Cleveland, earning a place in the Hall of Fame with his bulldozer-like blocking for runners Jim Brown and Leroy Kelly.

A FRESH START

X - - - - - - - - - -

The Browns began the 1963 season with a new coach, Blanton Collier, and a new approach to the game. Collier's style was much looser than Brown's had been. Instead of sending in "messengers" to call the plays in the huddle, Collier let quarterback Frank Ryan make the calls himself. The Browns rebounded to win 10 games that year.

In 1964, with Jim Brown again leading the league in rushing yards and Ryan pacing the NFL in touchdown passes, the 10–3–1 Browns marched into the NFL Championship Game against a heavily favored Baltimore Colts team. As the Browns' defense stifled Colts quarterback Johnny Unitas, Ryan threw three touchdown passes to his reliable wingman Gary Collins, and Lou Groza added two field goals to win the title game 27–0.

In 1965, as Cleveland enjoyed a superb 11–3 season, Jim Brown rushed for more than 1,500 yards and won NFL Most Valuable Player (MVP) honors. But after the Browns lost to Green Bay in the NFL Championship Game, the 30-year-old running back surprised fans and fellow players by announcing his retirement. Brown left the game as the NFL's all-time leading rusher; more than two decades would pass before Chicago Bears legendary running back Walter Payton topped Brown's total yardage. "It is possible that had Brown

X Although the Browns were famed for their ground attack in the 1960s, quarterback Frank Ryan's smarts (he held a PhD in math) and accurate arm made the team an aerial power, too.

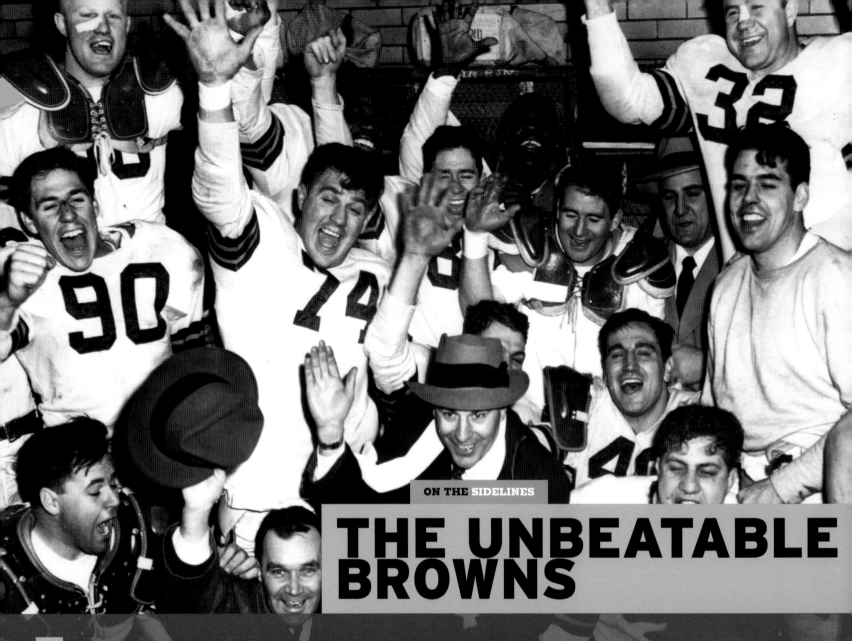

ON THE SIDELINES

THE UNBEATABLE BROWNS

The Cleveland Browns clearly dominated the AAFC. During the conference's four years of existence, the Browns lost only four games. But there was one season during that period in which the Browns didn't lose or tie a game at all—1948. After winning the first game of the season by a 5-point margin, the team won the next 8 by an average of 18 points each. Although subsequent games against the San Francisco 49ers and Brooklyn Dodgers were not quite as lopsided, the Browns continued to win. But as remarkable as the streak was, fans weren't impressed. As the matchups became less and less competitive, crowds for the games both at home and away began to dwindle. Fewer than 10,000 fans showed up for the season finale against the Brooklyn Dodgers, and only 22,000 attended the AAFC Championship Game between the Browns and the Buffalo Bills two weeks later. The unbeatable Browns may have been the AAFC's downfall; in the wake of declining attendance numbers, the league merged with the NFL in 1950.

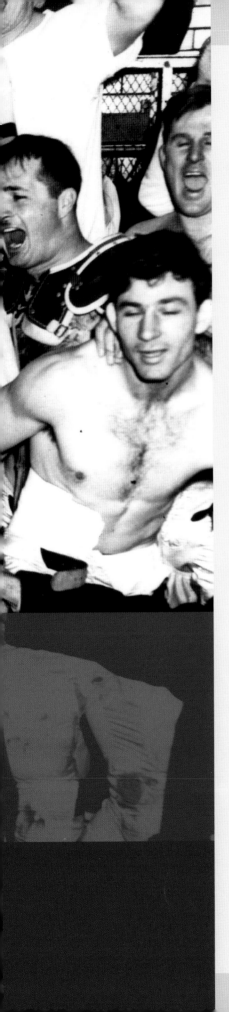

continued to play, he would have put all the league's rushing records so far out of reach that they would have been only a distant dream ... to the runners who followed him," noted *Sports Illustrated* reporter Peter King.

Even without its star running back, Cleveland continued winning. Leroy Kelly stepped in as Brown's replacement, and between his fast feet and receiver Paul Warfield's sure hands, the Browns made it back to the NFL Championship Game in 1968 and 1969. The sting of losing both of those games was compounded, however, when Cleveland also lost Coach Collier, whose failing health caused him to retire at the end of the 1970 season.

Although Cleveland maintained winning records and even made it to the playoffs in both 1971 and 1972, the losses of star players and a popular coach began to take a toll. As young quarterback Mike Phipps struggled to learn the ropes, the Browns recorded consecutive losing seasons in 1974 and 1975. Hope returned when coach Forrest Gregg promoted backup quarterback Brian Sipe to the starting position in 1976. The Browns went 6–8 in 1977, then 8–8 in 1978. By 1979, Sipe and the Browns had earned a reputation as a team capable of achieving amazing last-minute heroics. After dramatic, heart-stopping finishes to several games

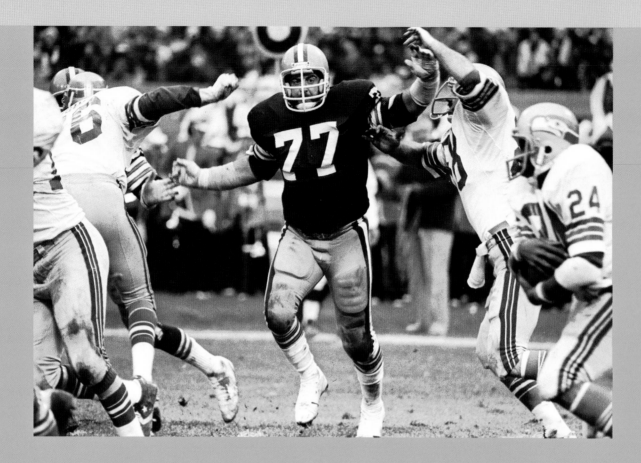

X Known for his hot temper and aggressive style, Lyle Alzado spent most of his career with the rival Denver Broncos but led the Browns in sacks in both 1980 and 1981.

during that 9–7 season, fans began referring to the club as the "Kardiac Kids."

The Browns, led by coach Sam Rutigliano, entered the 1980 season loaded with talent, from sure-handed tight end Ozzie Newsome to punishing defensive end Lyle Alzado. But Sipe was the undisputed star. Fans were so sure that the young quarterback would lead the Browns to the top that they began predicting a trip to the "Siper Bowl." Sipe didn't disappoint—he threw for more than 4,000 yards and 30 touchdowns and earned the NFL MVP award as the Browns won the American Football Conference (AFC) Central Division with an 11–5 record.

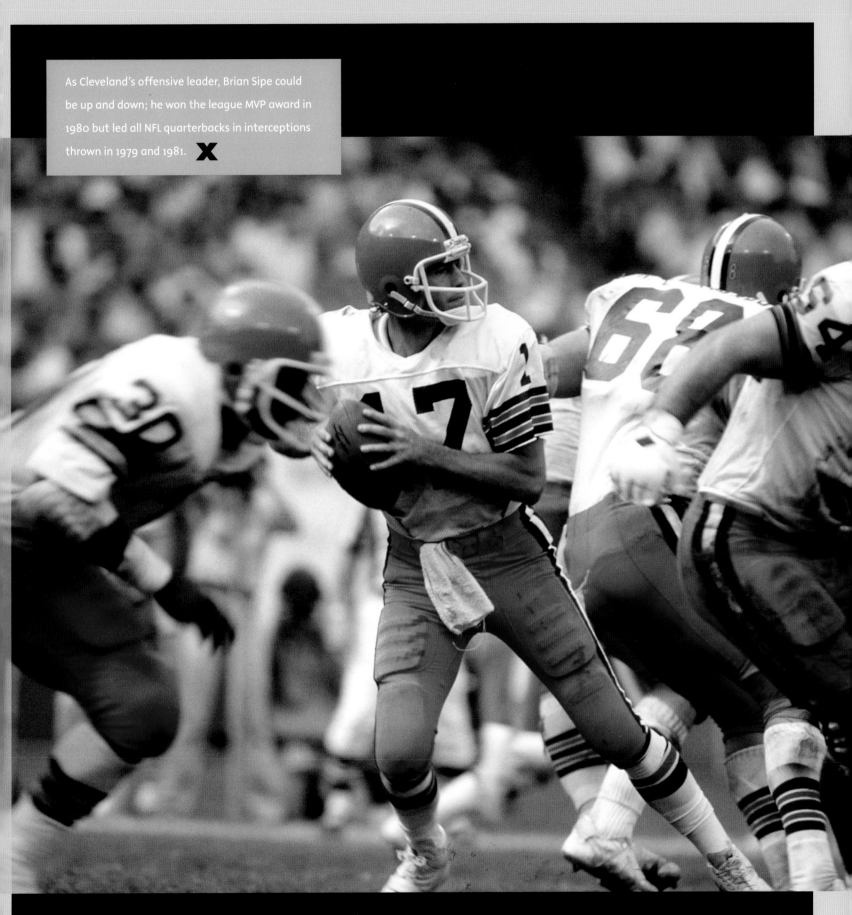

As Cleveland's offensive leader, Brian Sipe could be up and down; he won the league MVP award in 1980 but led all NFL quarterbacks in interceptions thrown in 1979 and 1981. **X**

LOU GROZA

KICKER, OFFENSIVE TACKLE
BROWNS SEASONS: 1946–59, 1961–67
HEIGHT: 6-FOOT-3
WEIGHT: 240 POUNDS

Lou Groza's success as a kicker earned him a spot in the Pro Football Hall of Fame and inspired the city of Cleveland to name a street in his honor. (The Browns' training facility sits at 76 Lou Groza Boulevard.) It also forced the NFL to make a new rule that prohibited kickers from using any artificial aids. Groza, who played for the Browns for 21 seasons and scored a total of 1,608 points for the team, taped up his kicking toe before each game and used a special tee with a long tail to lead his foot directly to the "sweet spot" of the football. Under the Lou Groza Rule, which was enacted in 1956, he was not allowed to tape his foot. But even that couldn't stop "The Toe," as Groza was known: He kicked a career high of 23 field goals in 1953 and put another career-high 51 extra-point kicks through the goalposts in 1966. Groza was also an excellent offensive tackle who earned All-NFL honors six times in his career.

That record secured home-field advantage for the Browns in the playoffs, which meant that any AFC team hoping to reach the Super Bowl would first have to survive the cold and wind of Cleveland Municipal Stadium—and be able to stop the Kardiac Kids. Unfortunately for the Cleveland faithful, the Oakland Raiders managed to do exactly that in the first round of the playoffs. Just when it looked as though the Browns would be able to come back from a 14–12 deficit late in the game, Sipe threw an errant pass that landed in the hands of Oakland safety Mike Davis. Even as the team's Super Bowl dreams ended, Sipe remained positive. "Yes, I have feelings of regret and despair about losing this game, but fused with them is the knowledge that we had a good year," he said. "I think we lifted the feelings of everybody around here."

Although hopes were high for the following season, the Kardiac Kids finally collapsed. Sipe's 17 touchdowns were overshadowed by his 25 interceptions as the Browns reversed their record from the previous year and finished at 5–11. Sipe left Cleveland in 1983; a year later, Rutigliano was fired as head coach. Defensive coordinator Marty Schottenheimer then took up the coaching reins, and the Browns started looking for their next star.

BARKING LIKE A DAWG

In 1985, defensive back Hanford Dixon ran around training camp barking like a dog. His bizarre behavior caught on with the crowds who had gathered to watch the Browns get ready for the season. Soon, fans in the bleacher section of Cleveland Municipal Stadium began wearing dog masks to the games and barking for their favorite team. Tickets to "The Dawg Pound," as that section has since been known, became some of the most coveted in the stadium, and the fans who sat there became known as some of the rowdiest spectators in all of sports. Some fans believe that they were even able to influence the outcome of a game against the Denver Broncos in 1990. After fans in The Dawg Pound started throwing bones and dog biscuits at Broncos players in the fourth quarter of a close game, the referees decided to have the teams switch sides of the field. That move allowed the Browns to play with the wind at their backs, which may have helped them drive down the field late in the game and kick a game-winning field goal.

HOMETOWN
HEROES

In 1985, Cleveland hitched its hopes for the future to quarterback Bernie Kosar, who had grown up near Cleveland before enjoying a record-setting college career at the University of Miami. Although Kosar was expected to be among the top picks in the NFL Draft, he wanted to play for the Browns almost as much as the team, who had a later draft-day pick, wanted him on its roster. So Kosar waited until after the 1985 NFL Draft to declare his intentions of leaving college. The Browns had anticipated this decision and were able to select him with the first choice in a supplemental draft that summer.

When starting quarterback Gary Danielson went down with an injury midway through the season, Kosar took over. Although he fumbled his first professional snap, Kosar rebounded to win four of the six games he started. When the 1986 season began, he looked like a bona fide starter, slinging passes to such veteran receivers as Newsome and Brian Brennan and to the newest weapon waiting downfield

Neither fast nor particularly strong-armed, Bernie Kosar instead relied on his accurate throwing touch (completing almost 60 percent of his passes) to become a Browns star. **X**

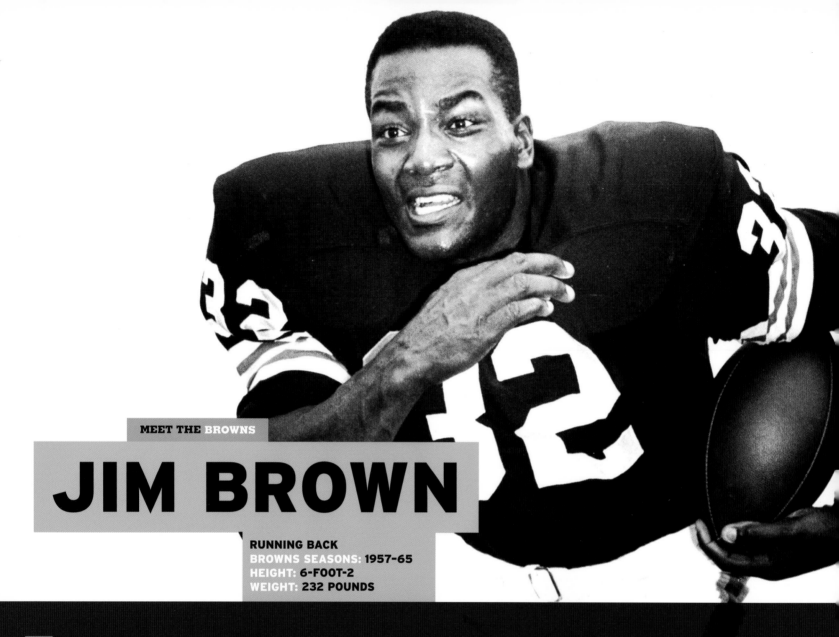

JIM BROWN

RUNNING BACK
BROWNS SEASONS: 1957–65
HEIGHT: 6-FOOT-2
WEIGHT: 232 POUNDS

Jim Brown's budding acting career was the only thing that could have halted the hulking running back's successful football career. In 1965, Brown was 29 years old and just 9 years into his professional football career, but he already held several NFL records. He set the single-season rushing record with 1,863 yards in 1963 and held the career record (12,312) until Chicago Bears legend Walter Payton passed him in 1984. Although many of the records he set have since tumbled, Brown remains the only rusher in NFL history to have averaged more than 100 yards per game over his career. Unfortunately for football, Brown retired after team owner Art Modell ordered him to leave the movie set of *The Dirty Dozen* to report to training camp. The multitalented Brown, who was reportedly offered 42 athletic scholarships in everything from football to lacrosse when he graduated from high school, went on to appear in several movies and later provided color commentary for mixed martial arts for him: wide receiver Webster Slaughter, who had been the Browns' top pick in the 1986 NFL Draft.

When the rebuilt Browns rolled to a 12–4 record and home-field advantage in the 1986 playoffs, Cleveland fans were confident that this would finally be their year, even after the Browns fell behind the New York Jets in the first round of the playoffs. Kosar led a late comeback after being pounded to

Despite standing only 5-foot-9, Brian Brennan gave Cleveland a big boost in the late '80s with his sure hands as a receiver and quick feet as a kick returner. **X**

MEET THE BROWNS

OZZIE NEWSOME

TIGHT END
BROWNS SEASONS: 1978-90
HEIGHT: 6-FOOT-2
WEIGHT: 232 POUNDS

In 1978, Ozzie "The Wizard of Oz" Newsome caught 38 passes for 589 yards—not bad for a rookie. In fact, those numbers were good enough to earn the young tight end the Browns' Offensive Player of the Year award, the first time in 25 years that a rookie had received the honor. But things only got better for Newsome. In 1979, he was named an All-Pro, and in 1981, when he made 69 catches for 1,002 yards and 6 touchdowns, he earned the first of 3 invitations to the Pro Bowl. Newsome played in 198 consecutive games for the Browns and caught at least 1 pass in 150 straight games, the second-longest streak in the NFL at the time of his retirement in 1990. But it may be what Newsome did after leaving the field that will be his most lasting legacy: On November 22, 2002, he became the first African American general manager in the NFL when he took over the Baltimore Ravens. He was soon widely considered to be one of the best personnel evaluators in the game.

the ground by Jets defensive lineman Mark Gastineau. When Kosar stood up, he was more determined than ever. "I saw a look in his eyes I'd never seen before," Newsome recalled. "He was not going to be denied. He was going to find a way to win that football game."

Kosar and the Browns did find a way, scoring twice to force sudden-death overtime. Mark Moseley kicked a 27-yard field goal to make the final score 23–20, the team's first playoff win in 17 seasons. But Cleveland's luck ran out the following week, when it faced the Denver Broncos in the AFC Championship Game. Although the Browns held a 20–13 lead late into the fourth quarter, Broncos quarterback John Elway was able to tie the game with just seconds left on the clock. Then Elway led his team to a 23–20 overtime victory that left the 80,000 fans in Municipal Stadium devastated.

Elway and the Broncos returned to Cleveland for the AFC title game in 1987 as well. This time, it was the Browns who fell behind, trailing by three touchdowns in the third quarter. Kosar led three scoring drives to tie the game 31–31 and had his team on the move deep in Denver territory when running back Earnest Byner fumbled the ball near the goal line, shattering the Browns' Super Bowl hopes again. "It's tough to come back and tie the game and then lose," Kosar

X Receiver Gerald McNeil earned a trip to the Pro Bowl in 1987 as he helped the Browns win the AFC West and march to the conference championship game.

said afterwards. "It's not fun losing this game, much less two years in a row."

As strong as the Browns were for the rest of the 1980s, the Broncos were always stronger. The bitter rivalry continued in 1989, when the two teams again met in the conference title game. But this time, the Broncos led from start to finish, sealing a trip to the Super Bowl with a final touchdown in the fourth quarter and winning 37–21.

That would be the Browns' last chance for a championship. Kosar's skills started to slip, and the early 1990s saw a string of four consecutive losing seasons, beginning with a 3–13 record in 1990. That season, Kosar threw only 10 touchdowns and 15 interceptions. Despite the emergence of running back

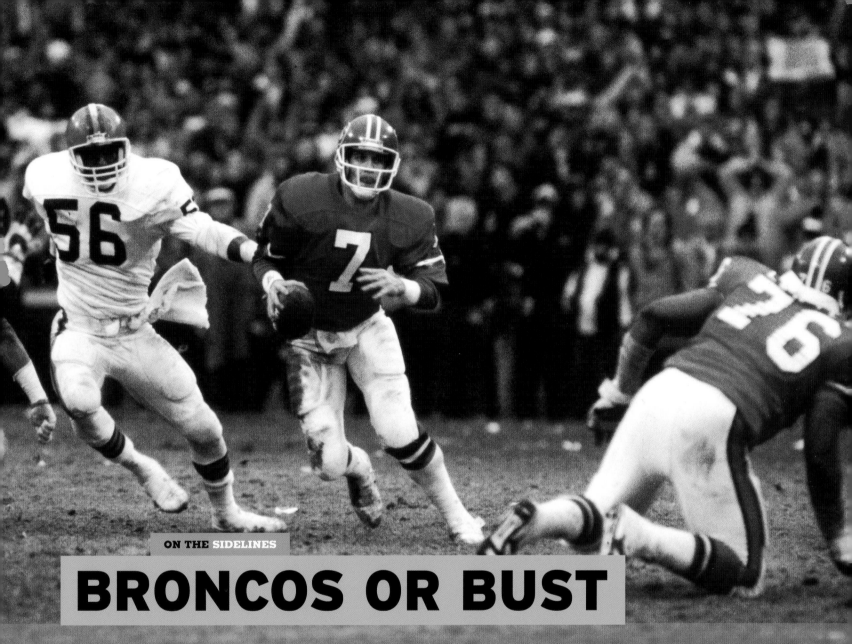

BRONCOS OR BUST

Only the Denver Broncos stood between the Cleveland Browns and the Super Bowl in the late 1980s. In 1986 and 1987, the Browns squared off against the Broncos in the AFC Championship Game. Both times, improbable plays made the difference between winning and losing. In 1986, it was "The Drive," a methodical, 98-yard march down the field that was led by confident Broncos quarterback John Elway. Elway took five minutes to get near the end zone before passing to rookie Mark Jackson for a game-tying touchdown. Then Rich Karlis kicked a field goal for the win in overtime. In 1987, it was "The Fumble": With Denver up by three points and one minute left on the clock, reliable Browns running back Earnest Byner took a handoff from quarterback Bernie Kosar just seven yards shy of the goal line. Byner was within a yard of the end zone when Broncos cornerback Jeremiah Castille stripped the ball from him and recovered the ensuing fumble. Four plays later, Denver surrendered an intentional safety to preserve a 38–33 lead, and the Browns went home disappointed again.

X Eric Metcalf was one of few bright spots in Cleveland in the early '90s; in his last three Browns seasons (1992–1994), the offensive dynamo ran five punts back for touchdowns.

Leroy Hoard, the team continued to disappoint. After sitting out much of the 1992 season, Kosar was released in 1993.

Kosar's departure upset many Browns fans. That anger increased as rumors circulated that team owner Art Modell—who was unhappy with the team's accommodations in aging Municipal Stadium—was considering relocating the team.

On November 6, 1995, Modell made his intentions official when he announced that he was moving the franchise to Baltimore, Maryland. Fan reaction was swift: more than 100 lawsuits were immediately filed, both by fans and by the city of Cleveland, which wanted to keep the proud Browns name, colors, and team history. Extensive negotiations between the NFL and city officials yielded an agreement that allowed Cleveland to retain the Browns' legacy, while Modell could keep the players under contract. The league promised to bring a new team to Cleveland by 1999 and to help fund a stadium for a new Browns squad to play in. Almost as soon as Modell left town, Cleveland started preparing for its beloved Browns to return.

THE BROWNS ARE BACK

X The reborn Browns used their second pick in the 1999 NFL Draft to select Kevin Johnson, who became Tim Couch's favorite target and posted almost 1,000 yards as a rookie.

In November 1996, Municipal Stadium was demolished to make way for the state-of-the-art Cleveland Browns Stadium. By early 1999, new owners Al Lerner and Carmen Policy had hired former Jacksonville Jaguars offensive coordinator Chris Palmer to coach the revived Browns team. The final pieces of the puzzle, the new players, began to be put in place once the Browns selected quarterback Tim Couch with the first pick in the 1999 NFL Draft.

More than 73,000 fans crammed into Cleveland Browns Stadium to see Couch and his teammates, including wide receiver Kevin Johnson and safety Marquez Pope, start the 1999 season. Although hopes were not high for the new team, many of those fans couldn't hide their disappointment when the Browns were crushed 43–0 by the rival Pittsburgh Steelers. The offense managed to gain only 40 total yards, and Couch, who was sent into the game in the fourth quarter, started his professional career by throwing an interception.

More than a month would go by before the Browns recorded a victory, a 21–16 triumph over the Saints in New Orleans. But Couch's late-game heroics that October afternoon renewed the team's hopes for the future. The Browns were behind by 2 points with 21 seconds to go when Couch launched a 56-yard "Hail Mary" pass that landed in Johnson's arms. "It's a memory I'll never forget," Couch said. "I can remember [New Orleans coach] Mike Ditka lying on the carpet and seeing him as I was running down the sideline. That was probably the best part of all."

Couch enjoyed the thrill of victory only once more during that first season. Things didn't improve much in 2000, when the team struggled to a 3–13 record. "I feel like I'm driving a runaway train," Coach Palmer remarked late in the season. By the end of the year, his train had run out of steam, and Palmer was fired, his two-year coaching tenure the shortest ever for an NFL expansion team.

With new coach Butch Davis on the sidelines and hulking defensive end Courtney Brown on the field, the Browns improved to 7–9 in 2001. The following year, Couch and Brown hit their stride, and veterans such as tough safety Robert Griffith and offensive lineman Ross Verba gave the team balance. With a 9–7 record, the Browns earned their

FANS,
UNIQUE AND YOUR SUPPORT THROUG
RS HAS BEEN EXTRAORDINARY!
N A GREAT RUN.
& CURRENT BROWNS' PLAYERS AND
S THANK YOU.
FOR BEING PART OF SOMETHING
THANK YOU VERY MUCH!

BROWNOUT

All of Cleveland cried on November 6, 1995. That was the day that Browns owner Art Modell told millions of loyal fans that he was moving their favorite team to Baltimore, Maryland, where state officials had promised they would build a brand-new stadium. Ironically, the very next day, the people of Cleveland voted to approve a tax that would have helped pay for renovations to Municipal Stadium. "I had no choice," the cash-strapped Modell said as he broke the news. The newspaper writers, television broadcasters, and mournful fans who camped out in front of the decaying Municipal Stadium made Modell out to be a villain who was looking to get rich quick. And indeed he did: Modell's new team, made up of all the Cleveland Browns players under contract when he left the city in 1995, became the Baltimore Ravens. In 2000, the Ravens won the Super Bowl, and three years later, Modell sold the franchise for $600 million. Cleveland's citizens eventually rebounded as well. In 1999, they welcomed a new Browns team to the $283-million Cleveland Browns Stadium.

THE BROWNS GO ORANGE

Choosing the uniform colors for the Cleveland Browns seemed as simple as saying their name. But it was Paul Brown, the team's first head coach, who suggested adding orange and white as complementary colors. He was inspired by nearby Bowling Green State University, where the Browns held their training camps from 1946 through 1951. The BGSU athletic teams wore brown, orange, and white uniforms, and the combination seemed fitting, somehow. But while the university's helmets featured its logo of an intertwined B and G, the Browns' orange helmets had no such adornment. In fact, the Browns' plain orange helmets are the only helmets in the NFL that do not include a logo. The Browns have worn a logo on their helmets only once, during a preseason game in 1965, when brown decals bearing the initials "CB" were stuck on as an experiment. Historically, the Browns have been recognized primarily by their colors. Some television networks that designate teams by their logos when showing scores or news updates simply use an orange bar when referring to the Browns.

first playoff appearance since 1994. Although they were up 33–21 late in the fourth quarter in the game against Pittsburgh, the Steelers scored 15 unanswered points in the last 5 minutes to win 36–33.

Injuries and salary issues depleted the Browns' roster for the next two years, sending the team into a free fall that included a 5–11 record in 2003 and a 4–12 mark in 2004. Couch began struggling, and, after being forced to split time with backup Kelly Holcomb in 2003, he was released before the 2004 season. His replacement, Jeff Garcia, lasted only one season. With Johnson and most of the other Browns players obtained in 1999 also gone, the five-year-old team was already in a rebuilding phase.

Before the 2005 season, the Browns put the team in the hands of Romeo Crennel, the 11th head coach in franchise history. Crennel had been the defensive coordinator for the New England Patriots when the Patriots won the Super Bowl in 2001, 2003, and 2004, and the Browns were hopeful that his experience would help improve Cleveland's fortunes. "The Browns are getting a good football coach and an even better man," Patriots linebacker Mike Vrabel said.

But Crennel had a long way to go. His Browns squad improved to 6–10 in 2005 before dropping to 4–12 in 2006.

X The Browns surged back into AFC contention in 2007 by going 10–6 and keeping their playoff hopes alive late into December.

BERNIE KOSAR

QUARTERBACK
BROWNS SEASONS: 1985-93
HEIGHT: 6-FOOT-5
WEIGHT: 210 POUNDS

It wasn't always pretty when Bernie Kosar took the field as the Browns' quarterback. He launched the ball with an awkward, half-sidearm motion and was all but immobile in the pocket. But somehow, he nearly always found his mark. Kosar, who grew up just south of Cleveland in Youngstown, Ohio, signed with his hometown team after enjoying a celebrated college career at the University of Miami. He completed more than 300 passes in 1986, his first full season as a starter, and racked up almost 4,000 yards. During the 1990 and 1991 seasons, he set an NFL record by completing 308 consecutive passes without an interception. As Kosar developed into one of the best quarterbacks in the league, the Browns became a postseason powerhouse, marching into the AFC Championship Game three times in the late 1980s. His abilities on the field and his friendliness off it endeared Kosar to Browns fans. Cleveland Municipal Stadium often rocked to the sound of those fans singing their own version of the pop hit "Louie, Louie," with the catchy refrain changed to "Bernie, Bernie."

With new starting quarterback Derek Anderson throwing accurate passes, offensive tackle Joe Thomas in the running for Rookie of the Year honors, and veteran running back Jamal Lewis eating up yards, the team was one of the NFL's surprise stories in 2007 and appeared to be headed to the playoffs as the season wound down. But even with a 10–6 record, it narrowly missed the Wild Card spot. Then, in 2008, just as Cleveland fans began getting their hopes up, the Browns started out 0–3 and sagged back to the bottom of the AFC North. Young quarterback Brady Quinn gained valuable experience when he was made the team's starter, and receiver Braylon Edwards had some big games, but it became evident that the Browns had more rebuilding to do.

But win or lose, the Cleveland Browns' loyal fans have rooted for them for more than half a century. As the city waits for its favorite team to return to the championship glory it experienced so often in its early years, its citizens can rest assured that the Browns will not let them down. Today's "new" Browns have the same hard-working attitude that made the Browns of yesterday great, and they hope to reward their fans with another NFL championship soon.

INDEX